Enough

Heather Varon

BookLeaf
Publishing

Presentation by *BookLeaf Publishing*

Web: www.bookleafpub.com

E-mail: info@bookleafpub.com

ISBN: 9789358368437

First edition 2023

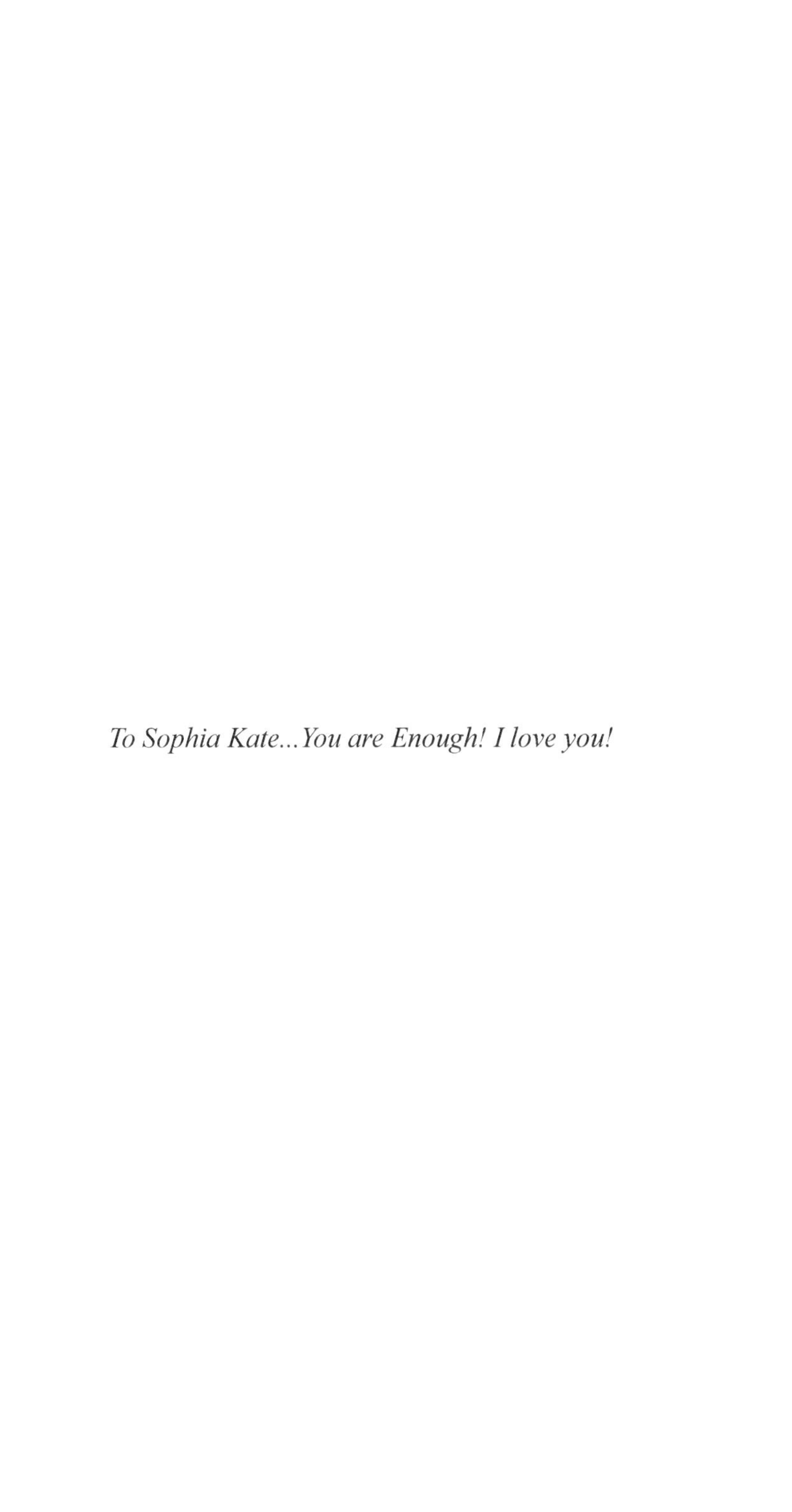

To Sophia Kate...You are Enough! I love you!

ACKNOWLEDGEMENT

Courtney and Kisha...for providing a safe place to land.

My tribe...you continually show up for me again and again.

Dr. Manisha Parikh... for taking the time to listen.

Tim Watson...for validating me each and every time.

PREFACE

The journey for healing does not have a timeline. It's not linear and follows no set path. The work is continuous. Many will not understand that you may look fine on the outside, but you are still hurting on the inside. Keep breathing because you are enough.

Heaviness

Sinking to the bottom
When you have no control
The heaviness
Sitting on your chest
Causing you to catch your breath
Holding your side
Weighing you down
Threatening to keep you under forever
Spinning so slowly
Then faster and faster
Dizziness swirls
Creating flickers of pain
Everything hurts and yet
Numbness becomes apparent
Creeping in
Nothingness engulfs you
From the inside out
Suffocating everything into blackness
No light
No movement

Waves

Waves crashing
A hint of salt in the air
Soft sand squishing between my toes
Seagulls dancing among the clouds
Dipping and diving
A cool breeze tickles my skin
As the sun shares its energy
Warmth radiates across my cheeks
Turning pink
Creating a peace
Only salt, sand, and sun

Unsettled

Hurrying to the next best thing
Wishing time away
Comparing
Causing angst
Never satisfied
Wanting more
Chasing more
Ungrateful
Missing out on life's joys
Dismissing others
Unsatisfied…unsettled

Noticing

Stopping to notice
A woodpecker landing on a branch
A red ladybug resting on a broad leaf
A white rose blossoming
Honeysuckle filling the air
Sweet and lovely
An effervescence of childhood
An orange butterfly fluttering
Spreading its delicate wings
Purple wildflowers growing in patches
Across the field
A gray horse trots along the fence line
Noticing the often unnoticed
As I run along the curved path

Soul Search

Deep dive into the abyss of my mind
Searching out all the feels
Tingling down to my toes
Breaking out into a cold sweat
Clenching my jaw
Jittery in the pit of my stomach
Tugging at my heartstrings
What's at stake
What's the risk
Tapping the brakes
Can't make the same mistakes

Made for a Purpose

Don't dim your light
God created you
Just as you are
For a purpose
Elevate and radiate
Your best self
Serving and loving others
Stay true to yourself

Dark Places

Toxic fumes
Swirling around
Gray clouds lingering
Web of lies
Self-doubt
If you can't trust yourself
Who can you trust
The enemy lurks
Behind every piece of trash
Fragmented heart
Uncertainty
A storm brews
In the midst of chaos
Standing in the eye
Of a hurricane
Seeking calm
Only God can provide
Shelter during the storm

Free in the Wild

Wind blowing
Through my hair
Feet hitting the pavement
Sun peeking out
Behind the clouds
Breathing
In and out
All the worries
Left behind
Each mile pushing
Demons away
Free in the wild

Twirling My Hair

Twirling my hair between your fingers
When you feel afraid
Seeking comfort
Only a mommy can give
Wrapping your arms around my neck
Squeezing tight
For a hug

Twirling my hair between your fingers
When you are sleepy
Scooching close
So I can feel your soft cheek against mine
Your breathing slows
Your eyelashes flutter
Drifting off to a peaceful sleep
"Mommy, hair!" you call out
When I make a move to leave
So I lay back down as you twirl my hair between
your fingers

Twirling my hair between your fingers
Your big blue eyes fill with tears
As they tumble down your already tear-stained
cheeks
Feeling sad

As I bend down
You reach up
"Uppy!" you cry
Lifting you carefully
Holding you closely
Your heart beating
In time with mine

Face scrunched
Lips pursed
Stomping your feet
Hands on your hips
Using your words
Frustrated

Twirling my hair between your fingers
My love is infinite
For your big feelings
Together
Forever

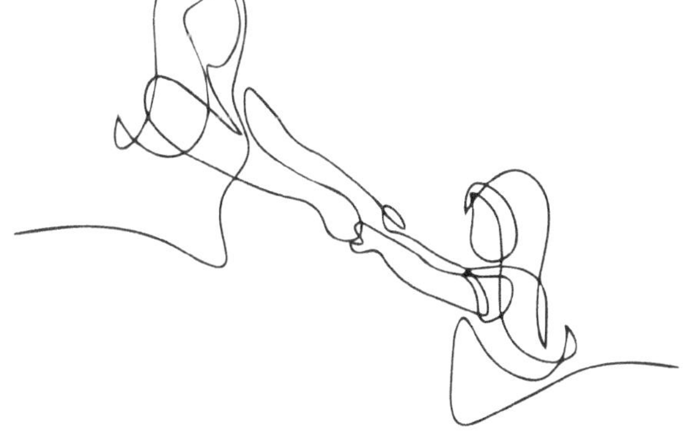

Kisses

Sweet and tender
On your cheeks
Forehead or nose
Down to your tiny toes
Blowing them
When we say goodbye
Calling out which flavor
Cotton candy...
Rainbow…
Strawberry…
Each one sweeter
Than before
Love your little lips
When they pucker
Ready for a…
Kiss

Treasures

What do you treasure
Stored in your heart
Memories flood back
With certain smells
Buttermilk pancakes
With maple syrup
My grandma's kitchen
The love she had for each of us
Abundantly generous…and
Could not be replicated
Even though we try
Moments in time
That matter most
A tight squeeze
With little arms
Wrapped around my waist
Sit with me a little longer
Undivided attention
Snuggle close
Time is passing
Ever so quickly
Let me store up
Treasures of my heart

Space

What do you let
Into your space
Whatever is allowed
Should be safe
Providing love and light
Peace and calm
Healing energy
Meant to help
Soothe the wounds
Created by toxic patterns
And vicious cycles
Repairing and mending
Providing a soft spot
For the soul to land
Back to its full intended self
Taking up space

My Soul Longs

My soul longs
For the cool mountain air
Crisp and tingly
Aspen leaves twinkling
Graceful and dainty
Dancing in the breeze
With the roar
Of the river
Rushing by
Shaping a path
Smoothing
Jagged edges
Easing sharp points
Of my mind
My breathing slows
Deep breaths
Of lush greenery
My heart is full
Peacefully calm
Creating space
In my soul

Inside Out

Vice grip on my heart
Tightness and heaviness
Just won't shake out
Moving in slow motion
Put together on the outside
But shredded to pieces
On the inside
A vicious cycle
Downward spiral
It takes every breath
Intentional thought
To crawl my way out
Not succumb to the darkness
Let the light flood
Its brightness
To fill even the tiniest of spaces
Until I'm shining
From the inside out

Pull Back the Curtains

Pull back the curtains
Who am I
Who will I find
The girl who's been hiding…
For some time
A fierce brave soul
Having slayed her demons
Ready to explore the world
Not settle for less
Than she was made
A powerhouse
With confidence and independence
Nothing can stop her
She'll shine like never before

Praying and Hoping

Longing and waiting
Praying and hoping
Even the smallest seed of faith
Keeps me stable
When the world wants to
Knock me to the ground
I stand firmly rooted
In God's love for me
His plans
His timing
Never mine
But always so sweet
And perfect
Just when I think
I can't wait for one second more
I'm given a glimpse
Of how much he cares
So I continue my journey
Longing and waiting
Praying and hoping

Not Too Much

It's not too much to ask…To love me selflessly…To adore me…To value me…To support me…To seek me…To desire me…To respect me…To pray for and with me…To be my partner…is to realize…it's not too much to ask.

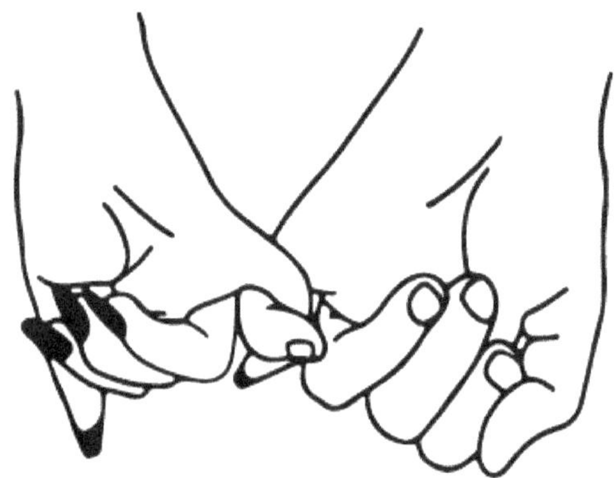

No Other Way

Wrapped in a warm embrace
Enveloped by deep thoughts
An inner peace swirls inside
Breaking free from strongholds
Keeping me prisoner
Finding freedom
Taking charge
Of things I can control
Making healthy choices
Versus poor life decisions
Gambling on a better future
For me and my daughter
Not settling for less than
What is meant for us
Paving the way
With strength and independence
Showing her
No other way
Than forward

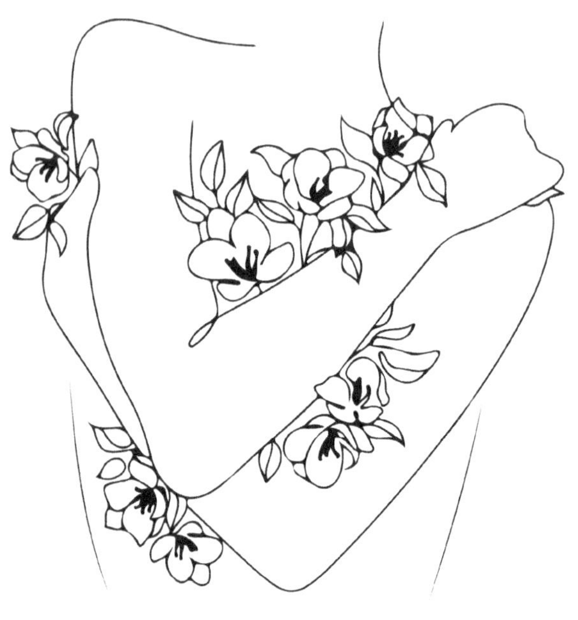

A Mother's Love

My heart will never be the same
All of my hopes and dreams
Tucked into the folds
Keeping promises
Sealed with sweet kisses
Your tiny hand in mine
A love like no other
Unconditional
Overflowing and pouring
Into your heart

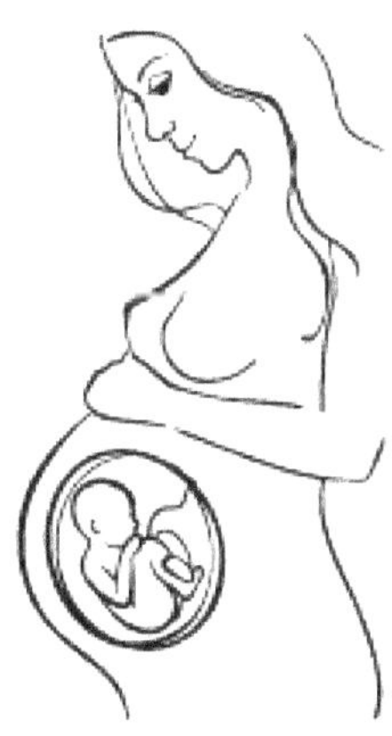

You Not Me

Months later
Wondering why
I should have said no
When you said yes
All your hesitation
Red flags from the start
Catch and release
More for the chase
I know what I felt
The connections real
The chemistry unreal
A whole other level
Nothing makes sense
I'm not going to waste
A single breath
Questioning motive
One thing is for sure
It was you
Not me

I Am Enough

I am enough
A daughter of the one true King
Royalty
A princess nonetheless
My worth and value
Too precious to waste
I have a lot to offer
Love overflowing
Passion for life
Grace and mercy
High expectations
Not lowering my standards
Wisdom from past mistakes
Enough to know
Meaningless misery
Time's too short
Not a second too late
To stand firm in believing
I AM...Enough